Zen in the Garden
Finding Peace and Healing Through Nature

TRACY J THOMAS

Big Moose Press

NAPLES, IDAHO

Interior Photos ©Tracy J Thomas
Interior icons ©Chris Elwell, Kurhan, Grzegorz, Japol, Windu from 123RF
Front Cover photo ©William Wang (123RF)
Rear Cover photo ©Wu Kailiang (123RF)

Tracy J Thomas/Big Moose Press
Naples, Idaho 83847
www.tracyjthomas.net/www.bigmoosepress.com

Zen in the Garden/Tracy J Thomas. -- 1st ed.
ISBN-13: 978-0692380574

DEDICATION

This book is dedicated to all cancer survivors and those who are currently in the midst of their journey. May your minds and spirits remain strong and may you find peace and healing in the garden of life.

Contents

ABOUT THIS BOOK

I created this book after several months of treatment for skin cancer. The experience forced me to slow down and reevaluate what is most important in my life. Ever since childhood I have loved to spend time in nature. It has been an important source of healing and peace when the world around me became ugly and stressful. Whether I climb a mountain peak or get my hands dirty while planting flowers in my garden, nature grounds me and reminds me of the beauty that exists when I choose to open my eyes to it.

My journey in this life has been filled with twists and turns. There have been many times when I have felt hopeless or lost along the way. During those times I have gravitated back towards nature, was reminded of my purpose, and began to see the path clearly before me.

My hope in sharing my photographs and words is that it will cause you to pause for a moment in your own busy lives and remind you to embrace the little things each day. That you will be moved to take the time to reconnect with nature and find your way back to the earth from where all life springs and to where all life will ultimately end.

Now go on. Heal yourself. Embrace the earth with your feet. Breathe in its life sustaining air and exhale all the manmade stress that binds you to a life unfulfilled. Open your eyes to the beauty that surrounds you and rest in the peace of those glorious visions.

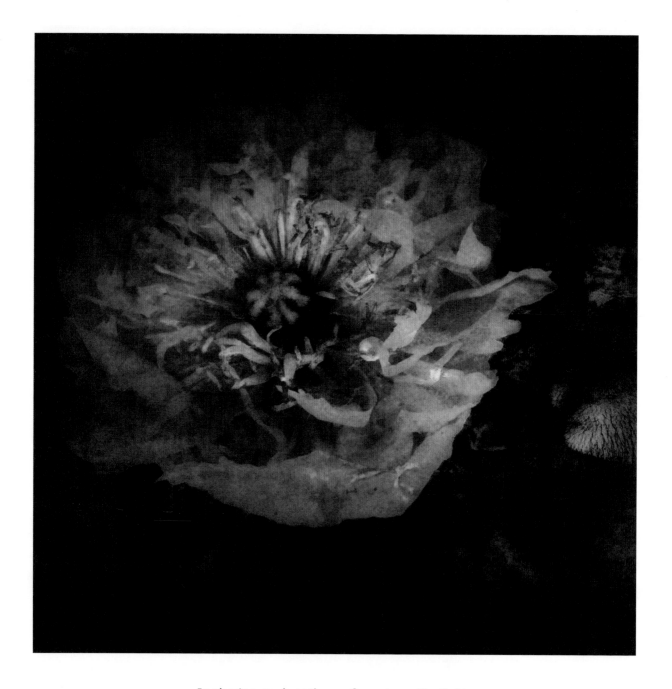

In slowing my breath, my focus is on the light.
With the ebb and flow of my inhale to my exhale,
I catch the changes on the flower's petals.
Soft shadows and glow from the last bit of sunlight.

1

Remember to Breathe

One of the most difficult things to remember as a busy and responsible adult is to breathe. Not the automatic physiological intake of oxygen that sustains us type of breathing, but the deliberate slowing down with a conscious deep breath. In through the nose and out through the mouth. When we make the choice to focus on our breath it is easier to clear our minds of all the clutter and simply be in the moment.

When we are in the moment we can begin to repel stress, cleanse our minds, and embrace the beauty that is before us. Nothing else matters. We experience the now. We let go of the past. We do not worry about the future.

Gardening Tip

Plant a variety of brightly colored flowers in your garden. When you add flowers to your environment they help reduce your perceived stress level, provide pleasing visual stimulation, and help you to feel more relaxed and happy. Make a point to visit your flowers every day and pick a few to place in a vase inside your house as a constant reminder to breathe and just be.

Like a child I hold my breath and formulate my biggest wish.
One big puff sends tiny white umbrellas to float off on the breeze.
They carry hope for what can someday be.

2

Honor Your Dreams

When I was a young child I spent a lot of time daydreaming. I had so many plans and hopes for the future. Everything felt possible when I saw it in my mind's eye. I had yet to experience all the negative thinkers in the adult world who seemed to live for squashing dreams. Whatever I felt drawn towards, I knew beyond a doubt was what I was supposed to pursue in this life.

As I got older I chose to let go of a lot of those childhood dreams for the sake of conformity and societal expectations. When I began to have health issues something inside of me was reawakened. I felt my purpose speak to me once again from that child inside my soul. The same one that used to lay on her belly in the grass, make a wish, fill her cheeks with air, exhale, and watch those dreams float towards the future on the tiny white umbrellas of a Dandelion flower.

When we choose to follow our hearts, we prove to that inner child they were right to believe in their wishes and to dream for what they would someday be.

Nature Challenge

Find a Dandelion flower, gather a handful of flower petals, or take a bottle of bubbles to the top of a breezy hill. Close your eyes. Think about how you have always dreamed your life would be. Embrace those thoughts for a moment. Now take a deep breath and a puff and watch those dreams be carried into your future.

Into the dark woods I walk with quiet feet.
The breeze tickles the aspen leaves in a symphony for my soul.
The shimmering chorus fills my ears and makes me feel whole again.
My fears flee with each new step and I am awakened to the beauty before me.

3

Don't Live Your Life in Fear

We know ourselves better than anyone else in this world could ever know us. We are each aware of our strengths, our weaknesses, our dreams, and our fears. Life can at times force us to focus on our fears. Negative chatter surrounds us every day. When we buy into that chatter we become frozen with doubt and afraid of the unknown.

When we choose to live our lives in fear we become convinced that the world is unsafe. We become paralyzed and fail to see the beauty right in front of us. Instead of a beautiful forest we see a dark, foreboding and dangerous place. We focus on the "what if's" and are blinded to all the wonderful possibilities in this world.

It's time to let go of that negative chatter, repeat the mantra "garbage in, garbage out," and take a step towards our fears. Open our minds to the beauty that awaits us there and trust in all that is good.

Nature Challenge

Choose one thing you have always been afraid of doing in nature. Write a list of your "what if's" (your fears) on one side of a piece of paper. Now write a positive outcome on the opposite side of each fear. Take a black marker and cross out each fear then read the corresponding positive outcome aloud. Now just go out and do it!

I sit with eyes wide open and I wait.
The miracles of nature reveal themselves in their own time.
With patience, nature's beautiful gifs far exceed the expectations of my soul.

4

Be Patient

Patience is a difficult thing to learn. We live in a fast paced society that has reached the age of instant gratification through technology. We have immediate access to our money, products, and information with the click of a button. We are a group of humans who have begun to forget what it means to slow down and wait for our rewards. This mindset causes us to overlook the beauty that reveals itself when we sit still and wait.

That's why I love to head out into the garden or into nature with my camera. It causes me to slow down and focus on the minutia of the beauty that surrounds me. I am forever surprised and blessed by wonderful gifts when I take the time to be patient and wait for what nature decides to share with me. When the small, beautiful things are finally revealed I am reminded of what is truly important in life. All the unimportant chatter dissolves in that moment and I am filled with a sense of wonder and peace.

Gardening Tip

You don't have to wander far to find beauty in nature. Plant flowers in your garden that attract butterflies, hummingbirds, and bees such as Salvia, Russian Sage, Chrysanthemum, Bee Balm, Aster, and Coreopsis. You can place a birdbath and bird feeders in your garden to attract a variety of song birds as well. The garden can be the perfect place to read, clear your mind, and to be amazed.

The seasons melt one into the other like the darkness into light.
Birth. Death. Rebirth. The colors change and remind us of impermanence.
The cycle of the seasons. The cycle of our lives. Change continues.

5

Be Open to Change

Change is inevitable. Most of it is entirely beyond our control. Nature is filled with change, some predictable but most not. The rising and setting of the sun and the moon are constants and predictable to the minute. The changing of the seasons may come early or late and bring with them death and renewal.

We are born. We die. Those things are universal truths for everyone on this earth but what happens in between is not. The in-between spaces of life are filled with change. Change is part of being human. Fear is what keeps us from accepting change. We can either spend our lives resisting change out of fear, stuck in a paralysis of stale constants, or we can learn to relax into it and accept the journey into which it is leading us. A certain level of risk is involved with change but the reward of making the choice to take risks are usually far more beautiful and life changing than remaining paralyzed by fear.

Nature Challenge

We are often creatures of habit, stuck in our stale but comfortable routines. Choose one of your favorite places in nature and do something there you have never before done. If it is a loop hike, walk the opposite direction. If it is a park where you usually read, fly a kite or collect acorns instead. If it is a lake where you always go fishing, leave your pole behind and skip rocks or go for a swim. Better yet, choose a place you have never gone before and journey there for a day.

Each drop that falls from the heavens kisses the earth with a passion unmatched.
The life sustaining liquid cleanses the dust and quenches the thirst.
New life springs forth where death was once a certainty.
The desert blooms, the prairies sing, the rivers run, nature breathes a sigh of relief.

6

Cleanse Your Soul

Rain has a way of causing things to feel and appear fresh and new. The musky smell of the wet soil and the shimmering droplets poised on a flower petal or blade of grass make us feel alive. Rainy days can be reflective and productive days. There's just something about the sound and sight of water that encourages a contemplative state of mind and helps to clean out the musty corners of the soul.

As a child I remember donning my rain boots and slicker and running out the door to dance and splash in the puddles. I would point my face up towards the sky and catch the raindrops on my extended tongue. I remember feeling so happy and ecstatic while I played in the rain. Why do we feel the need to stop those behaviors when we become adults? It is such a wonderful thing to do, this dance with nature. Pure joy should be the goal for everyone, whether child or grownup. It's past time for us to cleanse our souls of all that binds us to a life so unfulfilled. It's time to head back out and dance with the rain.

Gardening Tip

Place or build a water feature in your garden. Whether it is a small pond, a stream, or a fountain, the sight and sound of water promotes peace and reflection, will cool your garden in the summer, and will attract birds and wildlife. The addition of Water Lilies or Lotus Flowers will create a lovely balance.

Oh the wonderful glory of bees.

I watch as they fly between the flowers, content to gather pollen.

They buzz with an audible excitement. It is pure joy for their life sustaining purpose.

7

Trust Your Purpose

I believe that each of us inherently know our soul's true purpose. It is a matter of listening to and trusting that internal voice that has always spoken to us in the strongest of manners. We find it when we are able to silence the external voices who want to claim control of our own destiny. The ones who desire to mold us and push us into directions that don't always sing true to our own hearts.

When we cast fear aside and claim our own lives, we become free to follow the road that calls to us. We can recognize it by how joyful we feel when we walk in that direction. When we steer clear of it out of fear, we lack the same level of joy we did when we were on it. When we feel deep joy in ourselves we can't help but spread it to those around us. It becomes our purpose to embrace our joy and share the benefits with all of humanity.

Gardening Tip

Bees play an integral role in sustaining life. Without them it becomes more difficult to grow successful crops. You can help out the bees when planting your garden. Try to plant bee-friendly flowers, herbs and vegetables such as sage, oregano, lavender, poppies, tomatoes and squash. Place a small container of fresh water or a birdbath in your garden so bees can quench their thirst. Avoid the use of chemicals and pesticides, especially Neonicotinoids, to treat your lawn and garden. Help the bees fulfill their purpose.

The clouds float by in the pool's reflection.
I long to reach into the water and grasp one as it passes and hold it for just a moment.
I bend to scoop it up, but it is gone.

8

Stop and Reflect

It's so important to stop and reflect on our lives at various intervals. It is easy to get caught up in the day-to-day grind and forget to check in with ourselves. There are infinite demands on our time coming from multiple directions every minute of the day. Our ability to slow down and find a bit of solitude in the midst of this chaos is imperative. When we check in with our souls we are able to recalibrate the compass and find our way back to all that's important in life.

It's not necessary to take a lot of time or drive a great distance to find solitude. We can make a point to take short breaks throughout our busy days, to sit quietly in a garden or next to a pond or body of water and just check in with how we are feeling. When we don't have access to those places we can don a pair of ear phones, close our eyes, listen to peaceful music, and reflect on our dreams and desires for ten minutes. These simple acts can do wonders for recharging our souls.

Nature Challenge

Exploring new places in nature can open our eyes to the beauty of our world. Make a point of choosing one new place to explore each month. Whether it is the park down the street from your house or a high mountain lake, allow yourself the opportunity to reconnect with the natural world and recharge your heart in the process.

This is my path because my heart sings loudest when I am on it.
I trust the compass in my soul. This is exactly where I need to be.
I do not belong on some diversionary track that is dictated by convention.
Convention is not my truth. It belongs to someone else.

9

Trust Your Path

To make the choice to travel down a particular path is one thing. To trust this path is the right one for us is more difficult. We tend to over-analyze and think far too much instead of letting go and trusting in our intuition. When we learn to relax into our journey then we can realize we are exactly where we need to be for the moment.

When we follow our dreams, the ones that feel the most in tune with our hearts, then we are never on the wrong path. Every path we travel has something to teach us and moves us in the direction to achieve our dreams. It's past time for us to let go and embrace our journey with joy. Trust the path and know all beautiful things will be revealed in time.

Gardening Tip

Create a Labyrinth, spiral meditative pathway, somewhere in your garden. The spiral is the symbol of movement, growth, and change. When you walk along the spiral, notice the continual shift in perspective. This is a great way to clear your mind and to see things differently. Additionally, they create a beautiful focal point in your landscaping.

The ice cold cascade flows down the mountain with a force unmatched.
It settles into a quiet pool of green and slides past the rocks in its path.
This fresh, clear, life-sustaining liquid is strong enough to move mountains
and powerful enough to bring life to where there once was death.

10

Go With the Flow

Sometimes when we trust the path we are on, things come up in our journeys that seem to block our progress. These roadblocks are always temporary. When we look at them as nothing more than hurdles to test our passion, then we will find ways over, under, around, or through them. We should use these hurdles as strength and resolve enhancers and not dead ends that destroy our dreams.

Water is a magnificent force of energy. It flows in a specific direction and always finds a way around, over or through anything that blocks its path. Even when dammed, it continues to erode the banks and makes its way over the spillway in an attempt to continue its journey. No matter what steps into our path, we simply need to remember to go with the flow and trust our direction.

Nature Challenge

Go and sit by a stream or a river. Watch how the water flows around, over, and under the rocks in its path. These rocks are solid mass that would stop most things in their tracks. When we think like water we can conquer and even smooth the edges of the biggest, thickest rocks in our pathway.

The small insect flew past me in a blur just like it had a thousand times before.
There is beauty in its shimmering colors and a perfect symmetry to its lacy wings.
Each one a detail I was before too blind to see.
At last I am held spellbound, awakened to the tiny miracles before me.

11

Find Beauty in Small Things

When I was in the midst of cancer treatment I felt overwhelmed and developed a bad case of tunnel vision. I had to spend an inordinate amount of time indoors since my treatment was painful and made me extremely sensitive to sunlight. I missed going on hikes in nature and wandering through the garden to take photographs.

One morning as I looked out the kitchen window I witnessed a little Phoebe flit down from a tree and land on the edge of our fountain. Within seconds, it flew back into the air, dove straight into the fountain, popped back up and shook out its feathers. There was so much joy in that little bird as it took its bath. I had never before seen a Phoebe on or in our fountain and this little bird became the perfect, beautiful, small gift that I needed right at that moment in time. It was a reminder that no matter how unpleasant life may become, if we keep our eyes open, beauty will reveal itself in the small things.

Gardening Tip

Within our gardens there exists a macro world that is not always visible to the casual glance. Many of those tiny creatures are beneficial insects that consume the pests that do damage to our plants. Plant Yarrow, Dill, Angelica, Coriander, Fennel, and Dandelion to attract the beneficial insects to your garden. Beneficial insects include Lacewings, Ladybugs, Praying Mantis, Damsel Bugs, and Hoverflies. These tiny wonders play an important role in natural pest control.

Thick, impenetrable granite walls stop me in my path.
I can climb over them, but the walls are steep and slick.
I can hike around them, but this will add many miles to my journey.
And then I finally see it, a hidden crack that beckons and will lead me right to my destination.

12

When One Door Closes

To trust and travel our path is not always an easy thing to do. Sometimes we find ourselves standing outside a door that has been closed on us, uncertain where to go next. In those instances we often feel frustrated or confused. It felt like the right door at the time, but then it was slammed shut in our face.

As the old adage goes, when one door closes, another one opens. It may seem like a window, or a crack in the wall, but whatever it is, if it feels right and is open for you, climb right through it. If we learn to view a closed door as nothing more than a gentle nudge for us to jump back onto our correct path, the one that is our soul's true desire, then closed doors are a positive thing. Acknowledge them, be thankful, and take that next step in your journey.

Gardening Tip

Create an arbor or archway as the entrance to your garden. It will serve as a symbolic doorway that is open and welcoming and calls to us to pass through into the peaceful surroundings. Plant rambling roses, climbers, or vines on either side and train them to grow over the arbor. This will create a nice shady area for you and any wildlife that frequent your garden.

The light diminished. Detail, color, and texture blend into the shadows.
Faith ensures its glory will once again emerge with the impending dawn.
Bits of morning light kiss the treetops and chase the night away without fail.

13

Find Light in Darkness

O ur path may not always appear clearly illuminated. Sometimes life seems to fall off into a dark place that lacks color and light. In the midst of those moments we may feel lost and confused and have no clue on how to find our way back towards the light. These temporary, diversionary tracks are usually the result of listening to others who feel you would be better off doing this or that. We may give in and travel those tracks for short distances, but eventually realize we are miserable. That is okay. When we look at those unhappy moments as temporary, we realize they merely serve to validate our true purpose.

Each one of us deserves to be happy and experience peace. Not just happy, but ecstatic beyond belief with this life. When we stray from our purpose we can't see the colors, the beauty, and the light. We lack joy and live a mundane, run-of-the-mill existence. That seems incredibly pointless. Don't just exist. Trust the torch inside your soul and run towards the light!

Nature Challenge

Sit outside on a clear, moonless night and look up at the sky. The black sky is filled with billions of tiny pinpoints of light. The darkness is required to view these infinite, illuminated beacons of beauty. Sailors navigated by them. Astronomers revered them. Migratory birds rely on them. Rest in the knowledge that the light will always shine through the darkness to illuminate your path and bring you out the other side.

Little hopper on the blade of grass, you watch, you wait, you eat.
For some you are the arch enemy. To me you are divine, a most glorious conundrum.
A miracle of macro proportions with the ability to jump great distances with your spring-like limbs.

14

Embrace the Pests

Insects are often viewed as nothing more than pests. Gardeners and farmers readily use harsh chemicals to rid and protect their plants from insects so their crops won't suffer the scourge of these hungry little creatures. In our own journeys we often come face to face with the human equivalent of these micro pests. These are the people who seem to have their own interests at heart and who seek to use up every bit of nutrition we offer even if it results in our own demise.

What we don't always choose to see is the inherent benefit these pests provide. Grasshoppers can decimate crops in mere days however they serve as an important source of protein for a variety of birds and reptiles. They are also healthy for the environment with their nutrient rich droppings that fertilize growing plants. When we treat them not as the enemy but as someone or something that can teach us a valuable lesson about ourselves or attempt to recognize their value to the environment as a whole, we can then make healthier choices that support the entire ecosystem. Everything and everyone has its rightful place.

Gardening Tip

Avoid harsh chemical use in your garden. There are multiple natural ways to control pests that won't disrupt the entire ecosystem. Sprinkle diatomaceous earth, remove them by spraying with high pressure water, introduce beneficial insects such as Praying Mantis, and encourage bug eating birds to inhabit your garden by adding feeders, bird baths, and bird houses.

Be like a child again.
Kiss the earth with your bare feet and ground your soul to what is.
Squish the mud through your toes without constraint and smile.

15

Celebrate the Inner Child

When we celebrate our inner child, it is easier to heal. Whether we are healing from a disease or some awful injustice in life, when we find our way back to that part of ourselves that used to experience the world with such boundless joy, we take an important step towards becoming whole again. When we see with the eyes of a child, wonder never ends. Everything looks and feels brand new, exciting, and oh so possible.

When we allow ourselves to dance in the rain, marvel at the creatures in the clouds, squish the mud between our toes, lay on our bellies to watch a trail of ants, we begin to remember the important things. Our heart rates slow, our worries cease, our fears are diminished, and that moment is the only thing that truly matters.

Nature Challenge

Take a trip to the ocean and bury your bare feet in the sand, build a sandcastle, and search for seashells. Visit a lake and skip some stones across the water, fly a kite if it's windy, and collect pine cones. Climb a tall grassy hill and roll back down the side. Climb back up and blow bubbles. Think about your favorite thing to do in the outdoors as a child and go do it!

The climb to the top seems insurmountable.
Steep, wide, long, steps that make me feel winded and oh so tired.
Slow, deep breaths and baby steps, I focus on the final goal.
Finally, I reach the top and glance down from where I've come. Elation!

16

Baby Steps

There are days when everything feels like a struggle. Just like climbing steep stairs that seem to lead nowhere. If the journey was always easy, it wouldn't mean as much in the end. When we stand at the bottom and look up it feels overwhelming, insurmountable. We begin to question how we will ever make it to the finish line.

When we slow ourselves down, embrace the journey, and breathe deeply into the moment, we will begin to move towards the top with ease, barely winded, and in awe of the experience. Baby steps are what first taught us to walk. Taking baby steps now is what will carry us to the top. When we remember to place one foot in front of the other every single day, feel the earth under our feet as we do, and reward ourselves for our progress no matter how small, we will be that much closer to our goals.

Gardening Tip

Build a pathway to your garden and use handmade stepping stones. Create the stones out of molded recycled concrete and embed designs in them with items that have had personal significance in your life. Seashells from your favorite beach, marbles you collected as a child, imprints of leaves from your favorite tree, beads or stones from a favorite piece of jewelry, a photo or piece of art sealed in plastic. Each time you walk the path pause for a minute on each step and reflect on how far you have come in this journey called life. Feel peace from your past, live fully in your present, and be excited for the mystery that is your future.

There are days when I am blinded by the pale palette in my foggy brain.
There is white and there is black. I struggle to find the colors and the shades that lay between.
If this, then that, I see no other possibilities.
I close my eyes. I relax. I let go of false control. That's when I realize the colors never left.

17

The Shades of Gray

Everything in life is not all black and white. There are many shades of gray and colors that exist on the scale between these two extremes. There will be days, even while steadfast in our journey when things will seem a bit murky and unclear. Doubt can cause confusion and send dreams tumbling into the great abyss.

Those are the times, as we sit along the trail feeling battered and bruised, when we long for clarification and tend to look for definitive answers. But those answers aren't always so apparent. That's when it's important to allow ourselves to be lost in the middle amongst the glorious shades of gray and stunning wash of colors. Just let go of our need to control the journey and believe it will all work out okay.

The rain will fall but the sun will inevitably break through the dark clouds and brighten the day. The vibrant rainbow will appear to remind us that we have felt this way before but were always shown the beauty after the storm.

Gardening Tip

Plant a variety of flowers with colors across the palate in order to attract a variety of bees, birds, and butterflies. The more diverse your selection, the more balanced your garden's ecosystem will be. When you add color, it can also serve to improve your sense of well-being.

The shadows often linger there, dark reminders of the past.
Nothing more than illusions which appear to block the light.
We have the power to manipulate them, to give them a new shape.
We can shine a light on them and make them dissipate.

18

Love Your Shadows

The shadows of our past have a way of creeping into our present far too often. It seems to be a constant struggle for us to live in the now. We fear our future and run screaming from our past, over and over again. So much energy is wasted on these two actions. The noise our mind creates while focused on regret and fear, smothers any chance for us to enjoy the beauty of this moment in time.

When we hold onto the shadows of our past we give them an inordinate amount of power over our lives. We remain stuck in a holding pattern of guilt that forces us to relive those moments in a circuitous loop of pain. When we dwell on those shadows we reinforce fear. Fear that our futures will be filled with the same ugly things we experienced in our past.

It's past time for us to embrace our shadows and tell them goodbye. Our past no longer exists in a tangible sense so it can no longer hurt us. It may be a vivid memory but it is just that and nothing more. That memory can fade when we replace it with the beauty in the present.

Nature Challenge

When you feel fear and experience repetitive thoughts from your past, take yourself out on a hike in nature and go climb a hill or mountain and breathe in the view. When you reach the top, throw a rock off the edge wrapped in all the shadows from your past. Now say goodbye.

Your sharp, prickly barbs dissuade my touch.
Yet beneath your well-armored exterior lives a nutritious, water-bearing flesh.
And then I see it. A single flower sits amongst the thorns, bloomed and inviting.
It is a well-hidden beauty that encourages me to find a way in.

19

Lower Your Guard

At times it seems safer to walk through life with our guard up. We build walls and protective, spiky exteriors in order to protect ourselves from perceived threats and harm. This is due most often to past experiences when we were hurt or treated unkindly. Our trust has been tested and diminished over time due to circumstances beyond our control.

We spend an inordinate amount of energy protecting ourselves when in reality those walls block more blessings than pain. We sit behind the fortress but we still feel alone and alienated. The pain from those past experiences echoes loudly within the empty walls, glaring reminders of those uglier times in life.

When we lower our guard, when we take the risk to trust, the blessings are allowed a clear path to flow into our lives. There are many more kind people in this world than the few who are intent on harm. It's past time to lower our guard and trust in the good.

Gardening Tip

Cactus and succulents can make a beautiful addition to any garden. They are low-maintenance, drought tolerant, and some are even edible, as in the Prickly Pear. Most cacti have stunning floral blooms and create a unique habitat and ecosystem. Many birds and mammals eat the fruit of the Prickly Pear and bee, bats, and butterflies are drawn to the nectar of the blooms.

I have viewed ten thousand sunsets in my lifetime, each one of them different than the next.
As a child I was amazed. As a teen I was bored. As an adult I became too busy to bother.
The older I have become, the more I realize what I have missed.
I no longer have ten thousand sunsets before me but I will embrace each one as if it were my last.

20

The Promise

For every sunset, there is a sunrise. The stars in the Heavens are constant. The moon's rise is inevitable. We are born and then we die. These are the promises of life. Everything that lies between these things becomes our personal journey, our own story. What we decide to do with those chapters is entirely up to our imagination and discretion. We each have the power to write our memoir on that blank canvas in any manner we so choose. We can share it with the world or we can hide it away in our hearts.

The best promise in life is the one we give ourselves. That promise is to always forgive ourselves no matter what we have done, to embrace whoever it is we are at this moment in time, and to love ourselves for making the choice to continue on this journey no matter how hard it becomes.

There are no trial runs. This is it. Embrace life and run with it. Trust in the sunrise and the stars to guide your way.

Nature Challenge

Take one week to watch the sunset in a different place every evening. Take a photograph with your camera and write a paragraph about how it makes you feel. Each morning when you rise, sit quietly and look at that photo and read aloud what you wrote. At the end of the week lay all your photos and notes side-by-side and notice the differences of each sunset.

The surface, aged and weathered, worn and wrinkled, holds a beauty all its own.
Years of harsh exposure to wind, rain, snow, sunshine, have etched your form with grace.
You are no longer the tall, glorious tree that stood guard amongst the giants.
But a glorious sculpture from out of your former self, steadfast and strong, captivating and unique.

21

Aged Beauty

Along with growing older and realizing what is important in life, our perspective of self, primarily our physical self, begins to evolve. Our bodies inevitably age and everything begins to change. Our skin wrinkles, our hair turns gray, our strength wanes, and our bodies ache. This is all part of the natural cycle of life.

There is nothing we can do to stop this process. We can choose to accept these changes with grace and adjust our lifestyles to ensure continued health as we age, or we can fall into the role of self-pity and do everything in our power to resist these realities. But the things we choose to do merely mask the truth on the outside.

Aging can be a beautiful experience. When we accept these changes we can wear them as badges of honor for finding the strength and courage to make it this far in life. We can now wear those well-earned crowns of wisdom and dance our way down that runway on the final leg of this journey.

Gardening Tip

Trees are amazing. They provide shade, cool the environment, provide wildlife habitat, and some even provide us with food. The older they become, the more beautiful they are. Plant native shade trees and fruit trees in your garden and take photographs to document their yearly growth. Attend a pruning workshop to learn how to shape your young trees for healthy structure and long-term success.

There have been so many times in my life when I was envious of your ability to fly.

You catch the wind and soar there on the thermals, carefree and light.

One day I realized your freedom was never permanent.

You slowly and inevitably returned to the earth to rest your wings for another flight.

22

Back to Earth

We all, each one of us, come from this earth. In the end we all return to it. In the interim, we tend to become so busy we ignore it. Young children are very in tune with nature and the ground beneath their feet. Curious and inquisitive, they explore the world around them through their sense of touch, taste, and smell. Place a toddler on a patch of dirt or near a mud puddle and soon they will have it in their mouths, between their toes, all over their hands, in their hair, and up nostrils. They seem satisfied and happy this simple thing called dirt.

As we grow we are taught that dirt is well, dirty. We must wash our hands, wear shoes, protect our clothing, and keep it out of our mouths. We unlearn everything our instincts taught us about our natural connection to our earth.

When we find our way back into nature, back to the earth, our perspective begins to change. We notice things we have long forgotten. We begin to feel grounded and less stressed. What we thought was so important becomes less so. It is the perfect place to connect with ourselves and provide our tired wings with a much needed rest.

Nature Challenge

Find a patch of grass or a square of dirt in a park or somewhere away from a noisy environment. Remove your shoes and sit on the ground. Place your hands on the grass or the dirt and feel its texture. Feel the warmth of the dirt or the coolness of the grass pass through your feet. Close your eyes for five to ten minutes and listen to what it has to tell you.

Your twisted limbs reach towards the heavens in a peaceful, quiet praise.
A lifetime of swaying and bending to the pressures of nature and of man, yet you still stand tall.
The perfect example of resilience and strength, I can only imagine all the things you have seen.
I am honored to sit with my back against your trunk. In the silence, I hear your prayer.

23

The Prayer

None of us know how much time we have left on this beautiful earth. Not knowing can be either a blessing or a curse. It is a curse when we take it for granted and fail to live our lives fully by always putting our dreams off until tomorrow. It is a blessing when we realize the only time we have to truly live is right now, in this very moment, for tomorrow may never arrive.

For each one of you I offer this prayer. May you treat each day as your last one and embrace the life you have been given with abandon and love yourself enough to follow the dreams of your heart. Trust that heart and follow the path illuminated by love and your soul's very purpose. Know you are never alone on this journey no matter how dark it appears or how lost you may feel. Take the hands of those who offer them and help each other find the way. Celebrate humanity and the kindness that exists above all the ugly clutter. Embrace nature with your whole being and open your eyes to the beauty and lessons inherent in its goodness. We are all, every human being, every animal, bird, flower, insect, rock, river, and plant, woven intricately together in a giant quilt that is the miracle of this creation. You can rest in the knowledge that you were chosen to be an important part of the plan.

ABOUT THE AUTHOR

Tracy J Thomas is an award-winning photographer, author, artist, and instructor. She grew up in the beautiful Eastern Sierra town of Bishop, California where she spent her childhood embracing nature. She currently resides in Northern California with her sights set on a little cabin in the woods where the snow falls and the wildlife roams.

She holds both her M.A. and an M.F.A. and believes there is always more to learn in life. Nature is her strongest medicine and has always been her greatest teacher.

Follow Tracy
Website: tracyjthomas.net
Twitter: @tjthomasphoto
Blog: tracyjthomasphotography.wordpress.com

Printed in Great Britain
by Amazon